Karl Lagerfeld: Aktstrakt

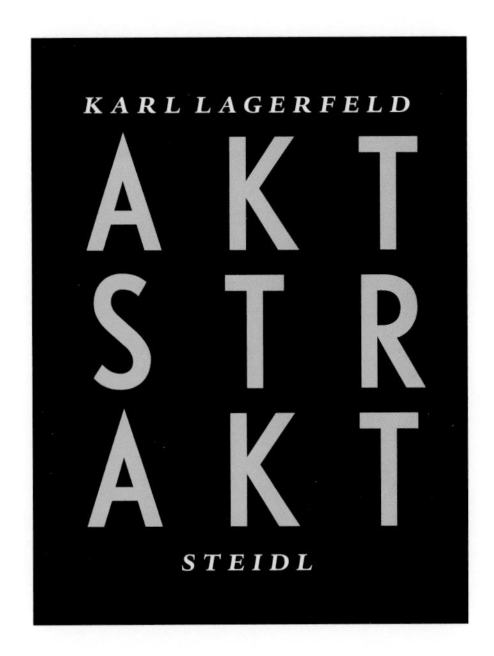
KARL LAGERFELD
AKT
STR
AKT
STEIDL

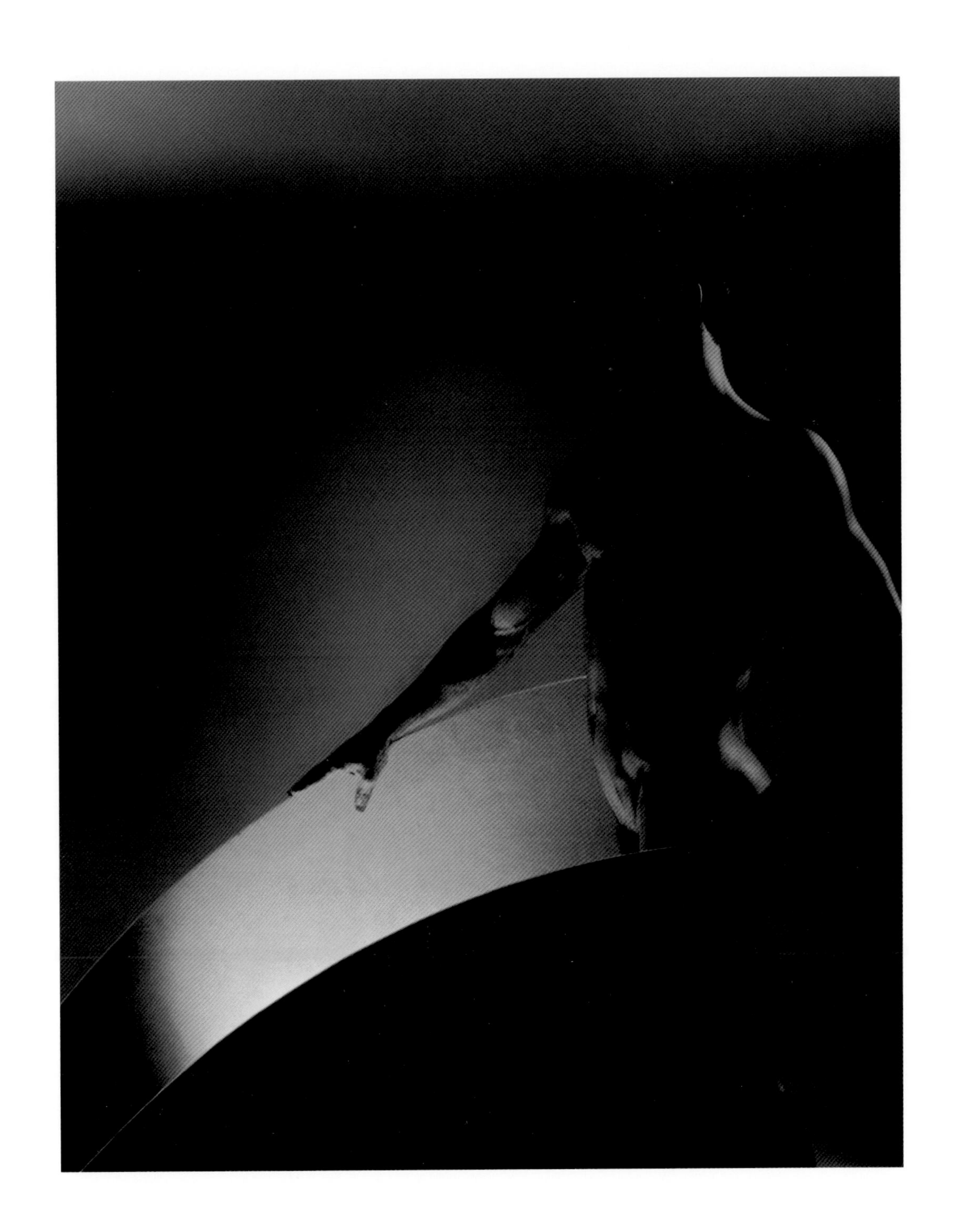

First edition 2000
Edited by Eric Pfrunder
Design Gerhard Steidl / Typography Klaus Detjen
Reproductions: Gert Schwab / Steidl, Schwab Scantechnik
Paper: Phoenixmotion Xyrrus
Printing and production: Steidl, Göttingen

Düstere Straße 4, D-37073 Göttingen

Printed in Germany / ISBN 3-88243-757-X